City of Stories

Denise Provost

Červená Barva Press
Somerville, Massachusetts

Červená Barva Press
P.O. Box 440357
W. Somerville, MA 02144-3222

www.cervenabarvapress.com

Bookstore: www.thelostbookshelf.com

Cover Art: *Somerville 12* by Steve Imrich

Cover Design: William J. Kelle

ISBN: 978-1-950063-51-2

Library of Congress Control Number: 2021948142

ACKNOWLEDGMENTS

Some of these poems were previously published elsewhere, in similar form:

ArtBeat, 2011 and *The Deal*, in Lyrical Somerville
Reticent, in Light Quarterly
Eagleton's Credo, and *Aspiring Poet Seeks...* in Ibbetson Street
Her Dwelling was Along my Way, *Strange Flights of Fancy He Describes*, and *To His French Mistress*, in Qarrtsiluni

TABLE OF CONTENTS

I Sing the City Eclectic

ArtBeat, 2011   3
Having Fun at the Festival   4
"Happy" was the Song   5
Full Disclosures   6
Intersection, Kendall Square   7
The Longfellow   8
The Bus Queue   9
The Thralldom of Stuff   10
Charmed   11
Pearl Street Ramble   12
Public Comments on the Latest Development Proposal   13
The Pasha of Elm Street   14
Magoun Square, in the Old Days   15
Requiem for a Home   16
Monday Morning, Porter Square   17
Historic Markers   18
Commiseration   19
Cleaners   20
Urban Satisfaction   21

Topical and Political Verse

Topical and Political Verse   25
Vocation?   26
A Cure for War? (2011)   27
Too Much Information?   28
The Pro-Choice Penguins (2013)   29
Bye-Bye DOMA (2013)   30
Grievances (2013)   31
Suspense (2013)   32
Money Ghazal   33
Lessons in Journalism   34
Calamity in Genoa: A Page 3 Pic   35
The Deal (2011)   36
On the Non-Assassination of the Saudi
        Ambassador (2013)   37

The Latest Campaign Offensive (2012)   38
Foreign Affairs (2015)   39
"Virtual Reality's Prospects Brighten"   40
Taliban Anthology to Be Published for English Speakers   41
Mad Men? (2011)   42
Theology for Patriots' Day (2013)   43

The Fields of Semiotic Sport

Eagleton's Credo   47
Aspiring Poet Seeks…   48
Reticent   49
No Delivery   50
Sonnet for Jason Strugnell (but not about him)   51
On Encountering the Master in an Unexpected Location   52
Transmission   53
Mr. Milton Reflects on his *In Quintum Novembris*   54
Father of the Prodigal Son   55
Sonnet Game Triptych: 1. Lady's Lament   56
Sonnet Game Triptych: 2. Begging Counsel   57
Sonnet Game Triptych: 3. Mariner's Request   58
Wordsworth Quintet:
1. Her Dwelling was Along my Way   59
2. Strange Flights of Fancy He Describes   60
3. To His French Mistress   61
4. For Marge Benjamin   62
5. Westminster Bridge, January 10, 2014   63
Walt Whitman Discovers the Internet   64
(Sic) Transit (Gloria Mundi)   66
Easter 1916, Reimagined for Maud   67
Ballade, for the Duke of Orleans   70
Shall I Marry Poetry?   72

ABOUT THE AUTHOR

To my late mother, Audrey,
who showed me that words were the best toys, and
to my daughters Emma and Eliza, who delight me

City of Stories

I Sing the City Eclectic

ArtBeat, 2011

Somerville, Massachusetts is a city of festivals and celebrations. ArtBeat, held annually in July, always has a "theme."

I'm at a festival, whose theme is "Red."
Ironic marvel, brought by passing years!
Epithet which accused, and summoned dread,
which symbolized our nation's darkest fears—

the color which once dared not speak its name,
lest it invoke Nikita Khrushchev's grin
or Fidel Castro's leer – face of the same
Communist enemy, poised to do us in.

But heirs of Perestroika are we now—
our enemies are somewhere else. Instead
of dreading Ho Chi Minh or Mao
we do not qualm to celebrate in Red.

With shaking of his now-cadaverous jowls,
J. Edgar Hoover's ghost peers down, and scowls.

Having Fun at the Festival

HONK! is an annual, weekend-long festival of activist street bands, held each
October in Somerville, Massachusetts. Its Friday evening opening event is a
Lantern Parade, featuring giant puppets, costumed participants, and marching
bands.

The girl-child drops a little toy into
her decorated lantern, candle-lit;
raises it up, so Dad can rescue it.
He reaches in, burns his hand; mutters *shit*.

Two men with babies sitting round their necks
hold onto toddlers, restive in the dark.
I don't think that your moms are coming back,
observes one dad, herding kids from the park.

It's late; one tired child flails on the ground;
her mother tells her: *just stop falling down.*
Big sister's ice cream slips out of its cone;
little sister rolls in, spreads a mess around.

It's over 'til next year! one youth protests.

Admonished: *Some children have no HONK!fest*

"Happy" was the Song

he played for me, stored on
his telephone, while others

were listening on earphones
and computers, dancing along

to its captivating tune,
reminding me of "Sunny" and

"Blue Skies, Smiling at Me;"
it's funny that so many

popular songs of happiness
are in a minor key.

Full Disclosures

It used to be, when someone walked around
talking to himself, I just thought, "he's mad."
But times have changed - now, when I hear the sound
of a solo voice declaim, I understand
that someone's talking on a mobile phone,
indifferent to others, who may hear
such stories as, how on a trip back home
he'd logged on to his father's computer
and accidently found a secret life –
some sordid messages and photographs,
until then hidden from his guileless wife.
Mom's now filed for divorce. I'd almost laugh,
but Dad's indiscreet habits seem passed on
to his obliviously blurting son.

Intersection, Kendall Square

The fellow in salmon pink
Bermuda shorts and
carbon-fiber helmet
breezes by on his scooter
past flocks of nerdy teens
in T shirts, eyeing him
with the incomparable
contempt of the young.

In doing so, they are distracted from
the man in the crosswalk,
bald forehead bent forward,
stringy ponytail behind,
whose black messenger bag
holds all the secrets
of the universe.

The Longfellow

The quarter-billion-dollar rehabilitation of Longfellow Bridge, spanning the Charles River between Cambridge and Boston, was begun in 2013. Scheduled for completion in 2016, the bridge was fully reopened in the fall of 2018, at a cost of over $300 million.

Unrecognizable, its towers down;
passage and portal still, but much reduced -
the Red Line's fine view of the Charles is screened -
crowds press down the one side open to use.

The span's named for a poet laureate –
the products, both, of previous centuries.
The poet's dead, the bridge deteriorates -
"under repair" stretching eternally.

Structural steel, each huge piece custom-made,
cannot be fitted to the aging frame;
each section here has settled, warped with age.
Better demolish it, and start again?

Each day that I traverse it, as I must,
its ornamental iron flakes off in rust.

The Bus Queue

Old and young stand in freezing rain,
await connection to our train:

two women, with umbrellas furled,
stalled in their journey to their world—

a skinny student lingers next,
gloves fingerless, so he can text;

his friend is next to him, perhaps
hunting through the "Where's My Bus?" app.

Hats and hoods swathe our heads twice;
some boots sport crampons, for the ice -

the treacherous ice, that claimed the foot
of she who wears a "walking boot."

No colors here but black and grey—
this winter's drained the rest away;

we shift from side to side, and wait
hoping this bus won't be too late—

it is, of course, now swinging wide
'round snowy mountains, where roads hide.

We shuffle aboard from the street,
greeted with a great blast of heat-

unwrap ourselves – heat's hard to bear—
our winter coats too warm to wear.

Soon we'll arrive at Kendall Square
where we will pay our subway fare;

and transfer on to points diverse,
MBTA's sad customers.

The Thralldom of Stuff

With tinsel in her beak, the starling flies
away to weave and decorate her nest.
I sympathize - I, too, have magpie eyes—
darting around, eventually to rest
on that which sparkles, or has a dull shine,
a shape alluring to behold; enough
to prompt me to pick up, claim it as mine.

Oh, what a truly wondrous lot of stuff
I've found, right in the gutter of the street!
A bicycle reflector, orange-gold;
a metal earring's rusty filigree;
a single smooth and slippery domino—
as connoisseur of rubbish, well I know
just how to be as happy as a crow.

Charmed

"Charlie Cards" are the plastic transit passes used by commuters on the MBTA transit system.

There is a stretch of Lowell Street where
sometimes, miraculous things appear—
one time I found a twenty-dollar bill,
likely because some dozy customer
had dropped it on their way to score
from the drug-dealing pair who lived
around the corner, then - the miracle was
that the cops bothered to shut them down.

Up the hill, once, after a heavy rain,
a drowned rat lay, holding, between its paws,
a Charlie card – only unphotographed
because I hadn't learned to focus in.
Besides, I thought, who would believe
I hadn't set the scene myself?
Or if not me (honest? squeamish?) why not
some trickster, who'd arranged this startling pose?

So maybe it's just one time I can vouch
that I've witnessed an otherworldly joke:
I ambled home, preoccupied with some
just cause, uncertain what to do, knowing
any resistance would be put down hard—
and found - that dingy sidewalk held Excalibur!
I lifted up that three-inch plastic sword
to fight my hopeless battle, undeterred.

Pearl Street Ramble

A hot night, no one wants to be indoors—
all congregate on sidewalks, porches, steps—
conversing there in many dialects,
the Babel-music of a cozy world.
In tiny gardens, big enough to hold
two rose trees, and a smiling, grottoed saint
moonlight reveals petals and halo-paint.

I wander past a building, once the home
of good friends - educated, cultured folk—
well brought up; financially insecure;
so genteel that they could not bring themselves
to recognize the "works" stashed by their door—
a cup of hypodermics on a shelf,
stowed by the tenants on the second floor.

Public Comments on the Latest Development Proposal

"[P]lanners are...tasked with creating public processes that are open but rigged....
public comment periods, community boards, planning commissions, design
charrettes, and a host of other interventions." Samuel Stein, Capital City

Lots of comments, the functionary said;
now it's staff's job to "sensify" the words
spoken against the monstrous plan. Unsaid—
the task of those whose job is to "make sense"
of irate neighbors' anger, their mistrust,
and criticism, is - *just play it down.*

Public meetings provide a chance to vent
against unstoppable forces of change
(or status quo, depending on your view.)
Grand plans of power will be brought to pass—
it doesn't really matter what folks do
or say; marching orders are handed 'round.

So, when staffers announce essential *sense,*
it's: *some objections – perhaps build a fence?*

The Pasha of Elm Street

How he enjoyed life, in that simpler time—
escaping indoor heat, sitting outside,
his feet raised up, cold pitcher by his side;
surrounded by plants, his pleasure and pride:
vining nasturtiums bloomed along strings tied
from porch rail to ceiling, then back again
at intervals, weaving a floral screen,
half concealing his chaise, where he reclined,
fanning himself - but always with an eye
for dubious strangers on the street below—
whom he'd halt with his glowering stare – so, no
house or car break-ins, during his reign.

His place, now plantless, is no longer green,
but tarted up, for tastes of those who come
to buy luxury condominiums.
The past, the porch, the man himself, are gone—
with his care of the street he oversaw.

Magoun Square, in the Old Days

Sordillo's Pharmacy, on Medford Street,
kept half the city dosed with Percosets
until the Drug Squad from the State Police
busted the place – can anyone forget?

Remember Frenchie? Ran the greasy spoon—
fried eggs out front, a meeting place in back.
If Frenchie didn't unlock the back room
you'd have to knock at Eddie Rocco's flat.

Regulars played numbers at Frenchie's place
or at the package store, or Drake's Café.
Wherever in the square your bet was made
there was one bookie, name of "Whirl Away."

Mothers would send their children "down the square"
on errands – buying milk and placing bets—
a pizza slice at White Sport, while you're there—
betting that number's only fifty cents.

No wonder the old timers miss those days—
all those familiar faces, harmless fun—
we've lost so much, adopting modern ways—
the chance to see real mobsters, with real guns.

Requiem for a Home

I never met those folks across the way—
I'd give a friendly wave, but nothing more
because, I thought, they simply would not stay,
but move on, as our neighbors have before.

You know how stories travel down the road?
It was discouraging to hear the news
that their landlord's mortgage, too, was foreclosed—
tenants turned out now, though they wouldn't choose
to leave so soon. They're packing up their rooms
while listening to music. Don't you hear
a great soprano soaring voice, that blooms
from out their open windows, like a prayer
that they be spared from this cascade of woe?

I wonder if they have some place to go.

Monday Morning, Porter Square

The homeless lady has a folding chair,
bright green, resplendent, in the shelter where
commuters wait for buses, or for rides,
talk on their cell phones, glance from side to side.

They wouldn't stop at all, but for the rain—
but would, to give her privacy, refrain.
They stand with backs to her, and she to them;
"There's no one here but me," each can pretend.

The travelers have soon hastened away.
Relieved, the lady of the house will stay
upon her bench-bed, with her handsome chair
awaiting some guest worthy to sit there,
or to entertain angels, unaware.

Historic Markers

The red brick house bears a blue oval plate:
Built in 1848—
yet before that marker came to be
its garden was home to an apricot tree.
We glutted ourselves on the fruit that fell
delight no plaque will ever tell.

George Washington's fort was somewhere near—
words carved in stone record the year.
Around the corner was the little house
where I washed dishes while you stepped out.
Our truth was written in years of pain—
trust breaks and does not mend again.

Abraham Lincoln sits in his chair
in a grand monument on the Common
where, drunk with moonshine, alive, alight
we climbed up on a cold spring night.
I still look for the scarf that I left behind—
a belonging I know I'll never find.

Commiseration

It was a kindly place, our neighborhood—
we knew each other, and we stayed in touch,
passing on news. Though none of us had much,
we shared our garden flowers, home-cooked food,
and gave rides to the carless. Life was good
enough for most, though sorrows always loomed.

We stuck together, fighting off the gloom
of bereavement and loss; the way we stood
with Millie, when her only son died young.
Helen had fallen and broken some bones,
so we had to bring her walker along
when we drove to the wake for our friend Joan,
who never had a bit of luck, said Flo—
as her car skidded out, in falling snow.

Cleaners

They appear around four, in uniform—
some nine-to-fivers don't know they exist.
Emptied wastebaskets, swept and polished floors
appear, unaided. Big buildings persist,
denizens come and go - but, staying late,
you get to know some of the cleaning crew,
if just in passing - others whom you greet
just exchange smiles, the way some people do.

One day I share the freight elevator
with a kind-faced woman I recognize;
I push a cart. Closing the safety doors,
she asks me what it's for. When I reply:
I'm leaving.
  Oh, that's sad - I've known you years!

I think: *I wish I'd asked your name, my dear.*

Urban Satisfaction

I walked through my old neighborhood just now.
It's changed a bit from what it used to be,
yet cozy still, beneath its fluff of snow.
The low clouds, too, pile up comfortingly,
enclosing evening streets with gentle hush
and concentrating all the restaurant smells,
intimate as my kitchen. I find such
pleasure here, in the city where I dwell—
crowds moving briskly through the dusk; paces
quickening towards home. May I stay always
here, living in slightly crowded places,
sharing familiar avenues and ways.

I'm glad I walked - this night is mild and sweet.
The very air tastes like good things to eat.

Topical and Political Verse

Topical and Political Verse

I was delighted when *The Nation* engaged Calvin Trillin to write topical verse and read each piece he wrote with pleasure. I later read <u>Deadline Poet</u>, Trillin's compilation of these poems, and was struck by how much explanatory prose surrounded each morsel of verse. It made me realize how quickly we tend to forget all but the most striking events, once they are not current, and only the most stunning scoundrels.

Such transience marks much of the topical poetry of the past. Marvell, Milton, and Pope, among others, wrote a good deal of verse about the politics and events of their times. These poems don't typically resonate with modern readers; they are often of greater interest to students of history than of literature.

I've tried to contextualize my poems by noting the years in which they were written. In some cases, I've also provided notes explaining the circumstances which gave rise to them. I offer them as historic artifacts.

Vocation?

All poets need a day job. Oddly, mine
consists of going up to Beacon Hill's
gold-domed palace, to try to undermine
complacent acceptance of rotten bills
when they appear, and narrow policies
that appeal largely to the cynical.

Success is all a matter of degree—
some think I'm wasted, tilting at windmills—
yet I'm compelled to question what I see—
a broken world, beset by many ills
-so little truth, even less clarity.

As politician, I have little clout—
but as a poet, much to write about.

A Cure for War? (2011)

When did our Peace Action stalwarts get *old*?
Why are our young folk not decrying war?
Is it because that, as they've grown, they're told
resistance is futile? What is youth for
if not to push at limits? I understand—
in their lives, war's been constant background noise—
in Bosnia, Iraq, and in the 'stans.
Why protest when the people have no choice?

How different when Selective Service ruled—
conscripted friends, prompted them run away
to Canada. Back then, the streets were full
of crowds: *Out of Viet Nam, LBJ!*
Here's one perverse thought - makes me want to laugh—

to foster peace, should we support the draft?

Too Much Information?

It started in her childhood, truth to tell—
she had a certain wayward way with words.
I hesitate to tell you what we heard
our little daughter say - it's just as well
her youthful voice had no great audience
for genuine mistakes that went too far—
that "vulva" was a costly Swedish car!

You'd think Health Education would make sense
of sexuality's confusing roar—
when she writes "necrophilia" on the test
for "hemophilia," how does teacher score?
She cuts the rind from Brie, and eats the rest,
removing the "foreskin;" but will no more
eat ramen noodles: "too much PMS."

Health Ed malapropisms are the *best*.

The Pro-Choice Penguins (2013)

For Karen Edlund

A crowd of Emperors waddles on parade -
from here one sees their banners: *Roe v. Wade!*
Uphold the Right to Reproductive Choice!
They would shout out, if they but had the voice,
about their own immense compelling need
to raise successful young - each mouth to feed
a hard task, on these unforgiving shores
along the Weddell Sea. If they had more
than one offspring at once, how would they meet
the challenge to keep warm, on fathers' feet,
one precious egg? Meanwhile, each mother must
hunt fish, relentlessly, as fathers trust
their mates' return; their careful calculus
for survival can allow no excess
of breeding, which explains their stated goal:
*Free access to **all** forms of birth control!*

Bye, Bye, DOMA (2013)

DOMA is an acronym for the federal *Defense of Marriage Act*, a law which prohibited married same-sex couples from claiming any kind of federal benefit, such as Social Security. DOMA was first rendered unenforceable in 2013 by the U.S. Supreme Court decision in <u>United States v. Windsor</u>, the occasion of this celebratory ditty, which can be sung to the tune of *Bye, Bye Blackbird*.

Pack up inequality,
marriage has
been set free—

Bye, bye, DOMA!

Government has
got to lose
interest in
whom you choose.
Bye, bye, DOMA!

Victory for love
and understanding;
SCOTUS has struck down
bigoted branding.

Now our future
looks more bright,
marriage an
equal right,
DOMA, bye, bye!

Grievances (2013)

To whom should I complain about this "managed care?"
Neither helper nor doctor knowing who I am
nor especially curious as to why I'm here,
suppliant in their office, in my woe and pain.
True care is something they might emulate—
meanwhile, their imitation care is not that great.

To whom should I complain about the FBI?
"Investigation" is no longer what they do.
Though offered solid stories, they don't even try
to learn the facts, but put it all on you
to find informants - witnesses, no less!—
though they love most criminals who'll confess.

To whom should I complain about our "leadership?"
Political high-flyers, perched right at the top;
a troop of puffing pigeons, whose decisions drop
upon us luckless minions here below.
To whom should I complain? I want to know.

Suspense (2013)

Our Supreme Court equates money with speech,
while voting rights have become obsolete.
The enemy comes pouring through the breach;
a mob is breaking windows in the street.

It's looking bad for our democracy,
as sequestration shuts government down.
The villain has the hero on his knees.
A zombie army overruns the town.

Corruption and obstruction rule the day.
The press collapses; leadership implodes.
Space aliens have a paralyzing ray;
they use it ruthlessly, as all explodes.

Will evil triumph, the End Times begin?
I've seen this movie – don't the good guys win?

Money Ghazel

I'm listening while a rich man speaks of money.
Sometimes it seems that all talk turns to money.

I hesitate to spend out of my horde.
What future have I if I don't have money?

The pleading woman lifts her hand towards me.
She reads my face, and knows I'll give her money.

When there's no work, what there is, is despair.
The landless millions ache each day for money.

I buy some peaches in the marketplace.
The vendor smiles – at me, or at my money?

My jewelry rattles with old, jangling coins.
Just decorations now; they once were money.

These sheets of paper tell me what I'm worth.
It seems a joke: abstractions equal money?

The wealthy merchant eyes the needle's eye—
might not the camel's way be bought with money?

Can't buy me love, and yet it must be said
that money, not love, buys my daily bread.

Lessons in Journalism

Reading these English newspapers is *fun*—
the writers for the highbrow ones can *write*.
There's content here; politics, left to right:
The Independent, and *The Guardian;*
the stodgy, serious *Times of London.*

Then, for the *hoi polloi,* the tabloid press:
The Mirror pictures girls in scanty dress;
and if you want to see a topless one
you'll find her gracing page three of *The Sun.*

Our *Boston Globe,* by contrast, is just dull.
Its page three? Some random mishap befell
somebody somewhere – join the lookers-on.

The proles like tits and ass each weekday morn;
our middle class prefers disaster porn.

Calamity in Genoa: A Page 3 Pic

"7 dead in cargo ship crash in Genoa, spurring investigation into captain," Boston Globe, May 19, 2013. This maritime disaster occurred 18 months after another, in which the Italian cruise ship *Costa Concordia* ran aground and sank in shallow water after a too-close approach to Isola del Giglio. The captain fled the ship; 32 people died, while hundreds had to be rescued.

What is it with Italians crashing ships?
Last springtime saw the island *rendez-vous*
between a cruise liner and ocean floor.

You might think that, chastened, the vow, "No more!"
would ring out in all captains' quarters, from
wet Venice to Genoa's ancient stones.

Instead, we read once more dismaying news
of yet another disastrous voyage:
the *Jolly Nero* slammed into a dock.

While rescuers dive, expert teams pursue
the reason for this crash, in "perfect" weather,
from broken bits, so hard to put together,

since ship and cargo all seem to be lost—
and, as if this mishap were not enough,
the *Nero* sheared the harbor tower off.

The Deal (2011)

In 2011, New England Patriots owner Bob Kraft and casino magnate Steve Wynn
proposed building a casino in Foxborough, Massachusetts – a plan they
abandoned in 2012. Wynn, in 2014, purchased a casino site in Everett; he then lost
his Massachusetts casino license in 2019, for sexual misconduct. That same year,
Bob Kraft was charged with soliciting a prostitute in a Florida massage parlor.
Prosecutors dropped this charge in 2020, after Kraft's lawyers successfully argued
that secret video camera evidence was inadmissible in court.

Crafty Bob and his good friend, Mr. Wynn,
woo Foxborough. They make a solemn vow
that the great Pleasure Dome that they'll put in
won't turn the town to Vegas - or Macau.

"Bucolic" is the way Foxborough will stay—
no high-rise buildings, or parades of cars
will spoil its hometown feel, or Patriot ways—
gambling will bring wealth, but leave life unmarred.

Since I don't live there, it's not up to me
to trust these wealthy gentlemen, or not.
I'll watch Foxborough's courtship, and I'll see
if their Deal, as they market it, is bought.

I'm certain that the one-per-cent must know
what benefits us masses down below.

On the Non-Assassination of the Saudi Ambassador (2013)

In 2011, US officials claimed they had uncoved an alleged Iranian government plot to assassinate the Saudi Ambassador to the U.S. One suspect, Texas used car salesman Manssor Arbabsiar - said to suffer from bi-polar disorder - pled "not guilty" in 2011. He reversed that plea in 2013 and was sentenced to 25 years in prison. Though FBI Director Robert Mueller said the story "reads like the pages of a Hollywood script," the U.S. imposed sanctions on Iran because of the incident. Many experts on the region question whether the Iranian government was involved.

You know that you can always trust Iran
to come up with the most nefarious schemes—
like recruiting a Texan car salesman
to kill a Saudi diplomat in D.C.

You think this plot was simple? Not by far—
that Texas operative schemed and planned *so well*!
Rather than ram his target with his car
he hired a hit man, from a drug cartel.

A Mexican cartel, to be precise,
since Mexico's convenient to D.C.—
restaurant assassinations add some spice—
Why be discreet? You could be on TV!

If you believe this tale, God help us all—
we won't need enemies for our downfall.

The Latest Campaign Offensive (2012)

This sonnet about the Republican presidential primary between Mitt Romney and Newt Gingrich seems now a quaint relic. By 2020, Romney had, surprisingly, established himself as a *mensch* among Republicans. By then, almost everyone had forgotten Gingrich and his election promise to establish *a permanent colony on the moon.*

I don't like either man, I must admit—
yet I read on, when press reports say how:
"Ex-governor turns more aggressive." Now
it makes me wonder, will the Newt get bit
by the man (not his mutt) who's known as Mitt?
Since "Romney, Gingrich clash in Florida"
makes me envision wrestlers in the raw
or even gladiators in a pit.

The papers say that Mitt's "reengineered"—
is he perhaps a Dalek or android?
Created to inflict pain, without fear,
he skewers his foe in all the day's tabloids—
mocking Newt's longed-for lunar colony.
(This contest's end will leave us with a void.)

Foreign Affairs (2015)

I don't remember the specific news stories that day, but just reading the newspapers gave rise to this image of the world as an intimate, gossipy community.

Ukraine turned up with a black eye, and worse—
Russia prevaricated – *wasn't me!* –
made excuses, laying all blame elsewhere.
Around our neighborhood, folks disbelieved;
on viewing Putin's bare chest, saw instead
a white string vest, and muttered *wife-beater.*

Nobody really knew the Arab lads,
which was a shame – there were so many, now—
though barely out of adolescence. Tall
and loud as men, demeanor serious—
yet few could understand their gutturals
and strung-on vowels, their tones of insistence.

Then, there's that unexpected couple:
fastidious Japan – careful, precise—
now dating India! Charming, of course,
but, oh, his family - large, unruly
argumentative lot. Yet there the two sit,
besotted, holding hands and drinking tea.

"Virtual Reality's Prospects Brighten"

"the Oculus Rift…envelops the vision of people who wear it in vivid, three-dimensional images…. Cliff Bleszinski …said that the first time he wore the rift headset, 'I gazed into the abyss, and the abyss gazed back at me.'" Boston Globe, Feb. 16, 2013.

Reality has *so* become passé—
please recognize: reality's been *done*.
We're eager to discover other ways
to craft contexts in which we can have fun.

Let's try imitation reality,
improving upon what's already here;
as for dimensions, we can start with three
for now; we'll add a fourth when we know where
to put it. In our new Oculus Rift
headset - into which we fix eager eyes—
we're keen as those who gazed on the abyss,
and saw it gazing back - we realize
it protects us from any real abyss
to have a substitute, that's artifice.

"Taliban Anthology to Be Published for English Speakers, or
The Black-Turbaned Wilfred Owens of Wardak" **(Huffington**
Post headline, on a story from the Associated Press, May 6,
2012)

I will confess: I haven't tried too hard
to understand the Taliban. But now
a door is opening, to show me how

I might gain insight. Words of soldier-bards
collected, translated; their hearts laid bare—
who would have thought to find a work so rare?

"Their verse is fervent," it is said. They are
"deeply emotional people." Aren't we all?
And isn't that just what the point will be?

Because, although the Taliban seem far
from us in world view, sensibility,
belief – what do we share, if not humanity?

Politicians, mullahs are bound to fall,
and warlords, too. Poetry outlasts all.

Mad Men? (2011)

Allen West was a Republican Congressman from Florida, 2011-2013. In 2011, he told Fox News that the Democratic Party is a "21st-century plantation," adding: "I'm here as the modern-day Harriet Tubman, to kind of lead people...away from that plantation...." West's claim that scores of his Congressional colleagues were *Communists* didn't even make it into lists of his most outrageous public statements (e.g., Think Progress, February 16, 2012; Politico, April 6, 2012.)

Why resurrect the 50's zeitgeist now?
Who has nostalgia for those dreary years
when people, straight-jacketed by their fears,

viewed neighbors with suspicion? Is that how
we want to live? All the martinis in
the world can't blur such a default of reason.

Our past's not past - it's left us well endowed.
Congressman Allen West, of Florida,
says eighty-one members of Congress are

Communists. Just enter the blogosphere
to hear the new McCarthyism's rants
as it panders towards its fond audience.

Republicans declare open season
on that bane of smug and sour clerics,
"*artificial* birth control." Hysterics

spread across our vast, secular nation:
self-styled patriots speak of being *free*
while trying to extinguish liberty.

Theology for Patriots' Day (2013)

After lunch we sat for a while and talked.
You told me, *God's an absentee landlord*
-a remark that could get a priest defrocked -
but perhaps kinder than to say, *He's bored
and toys with us.* He sees us beg for food
or experiments on us with disease;
then, as we suffer, rates our attitude
searches our prayers for *thank you* and for *please.*

Perhaps our world is shabby with neglect
and we're poor stewards, and not always kind.
What could it be but malice, though, which wrecked
the marathon, took lives, with a device
designed to blow off people's legs and feet?
Did Satan take a stroll down Boylston Street?

The Fields of Semiotic Sport

Eagleton's Credo

"Poetry is a superior form of babbling." Terry Eagleton, How to Read a Poem

Just by existing, Poetry fulfills
our deeply held Utopian desires
-a form of life that's not so much in thrall
to duty, but turns obligation's call
back towards indulgence of our wayward will
to flirt among unattached signifiers.

Suspend your grim, communicative labors!
Come to the fields of semiotic sport
where sound and meaning recklessly cavort.

Lofty Poetry covets its neighbor's
wife, its house, servant, its horse and cart.
Freed from loveless marriage to one meaning,
Poetry is superior babbling,
convincing us that antic play is Art.

Aspiring Poet Seeks...

We know the Muses are all female, right?
That's why men write most of our poetry.
I'm searching for a muse who's just my type
and wants to spend quality time with me.

A lissome redhead tempted me, but then
came the deal-breaker: she smoked cigarettes.
A blonde Madonna whispered to me; when
I turned, she'd become a heartless coquette.

There was a dark one once, with smudgy eyes,
whose heavy-lidded look was eloquent.
I leaned in closer, quick to sympathize,
but she strolled off with some loquacious gent.

I can't compete with Masculinity—
I don't think the Muses will sing to me.

Reticent

Emotion's an unappetizing platter,
filled up with squishy innards, slime, and slugs—
or worse, with sentimental subject matter
like birthday parties, puppy dogs, and hugs.

I'll take a place among the sober Stoics
and light my lamp to shine upon Ideas;
illuminate some genuine heroics
or place a humorous mask on top of tears.

I've no wish to make a display of feelings
in poetry – it offends self-restraint.
I wouldn't want to talk about the dealings
that life has dealt – for indiscreet, I ain't.

I must reject the thought that poet's art
subordinates the head to a foolish heart.

No Delivery

"The wicked in Gehenna lie on their beds of nails, and wait for mail."
Isaac Bashevis Singer

I doubted I would ever make the cut.
Lacking in virtue, I'd need special grace
to keep me out of that infernal place
the nuns warned us about – picturesque, but
not a choice spot to spend eternity.
It was with ample measure of chagrin
I found myself being escorted in
to classic Dante-esque topography.

I'm more or less resigned to being here.
I couldn't squelch the impulse to transgress,
but if I'd left a forwarding address
I could at least hope postcards would appear
sometimes. Too late - I lived life as a rogue—
and now, I'd sell my soul to receive *Vogue*.

Sonnet for Jason Strugnell (but not about him)

Jason Strugnell is a fictitious poet, invented by the English poet Wendy Cope. "He began as a joke to amuse a friend," Cope writes in the notes to her 2008 collection, Two Cures for Love, "and then started to get published." Many of the Strugnell poems are in Cope's 1986 book, Making Cocoa for Kingsley Amis.

If I compare you to a summer's day,
perhaps it oughtn't be an English one—
my similies could quickly go astray,
and liken you to fog, not to the sun.

But since your heart is all inconstancy,
the English summer is a trope that's apt.
I rise up, smiling, to enjoy the sea,
but don't go bathing, since the weather's crap.

I'd better face the fact: your love's grown cold—
so, once again, chill metaphor will serve.
This verse is wooly jumper for my soul—
I would just dump you if I had the nerve.

Shakespearean sonnets may be overdone,
but writing them is such a lot of fun.

On Encountering the Master in an Unexpected Location

There are at least four English-language Facebook pages for Rumi, and at least one Facebook group. Anyone can be a Follower!

Do you not think it strange, immortal sage—
great poet, mystic, devotee of God -
to find that you possess a Facebook page?
I must confess that I still find it odd
that you, who died in twelve-seventy-three,
would reassert your powers to pursue
a social network through technology.

Somehow, this ambit doesn't seem like you;
and "public figure" - isn't that a stretch?
I can't imagine you'd describe your role
in this way. I don't like to be a *kvetch*,
but I would designate you as "Great Soul."
Yet there you are, online, and in the end,
I don't mind saying, "Rumi is my Friend."

Transcription

Transmission

"Rumi is God's funny family on a big open radio line." Coleman Barks, non-
Persian-speaking "translator" of Rumi's poetry into English

Tune in, devoted one, we start at dawn—
still stuffed with dreams, we wonder where we've been
and marvel how the sun shines on the scene,
while we struggle to comprehend birdsong.
Patterns of leafy shadows now grow long,
as our illumination hurries west.

But radio transmissions do not rest.
Along the line, ten million lights flash on:
Are you there? Do you remember? Are we
still connected? Listen! Love's at the door;
love is the door, the open air, the sea—
its message floats in bottles, in the roar
of vast sky charged with electricity—
want to flee from this funny family?

Mr. Milton Reflects on his *In Quintum Novembris*

On November 5, 1605, Guy Fawkes and eight other men were caught preparing to explode a quantity of gunpowder under the Houses of Parliament and were subsequently executed. Parliament decreed celebration of "an annual and constant memorial of that day." In John Milton's time, festivities included original epic poetry; he composed "On the Fifth of November" in Latin, at age 17.

It was an early poem of mine, yet filled
with all the dazzle which would bring me fame;
attuned to my time's proper sentiments:
joy and relief – the Romish plot is foiled!

Fawkes seized, and dragged to painful punishments!
Our Parliament acts to honor the day
in perpetuity. Hear the laments
of the treacherous, fearful when they see
genial bonfires lighting gleeful streets.

My educated friends spout admiration
for words that I've composed in celebration.
Had I but used English, I would have reached
the masses with my lofty erudition
to prove my point: Popery is perdition!

Father of the Prodigal Son

Don't think that I'm oblivious to the
tensions simmering among the sauces—
yet any feeling father would have done
the same thing - such reversal of losses!

This son of mine was dead and now he lives.
My hope had bled away, and then I saw
him hesitating there – why not forgive
when its sweet relief fulfills divine law?

My heart and spirit flew to him as one.
He spoke to me with such humility:
"No longer worthy to be called your son."
I embraced him, called for festivities.

Now one son must forgive himself. The other
must reconcile to love, again, his brother.

Sonnet Game Triptych: 1. Lady's Lament

I wrote the following three poems to play The Sonnet Game - which I did not invent. This entertainment was devised by my daughter Emma and her best friend at Somerville High School. I wasn't let in on the game until years after they graduated. The rules are these: a round starts with one person assuming the persona of a character in a work of fiction. Using that character's voice, the writer then poses a problem or question from the fiction in the form of a sonnet. The other player then replies, in sonnet form, preferably with patronizing, know-it-all advice.

My lord, I've heard you are a gentleman
whose kindly wisdom can set wrongs aright;
who helps the lost and troubled when he can—
pray, sir, shine some small brightness in my night.

My erstwhile lover is Denmark's fair prince;
of his devotion, I had once no doubt.
Can you explain what change has gripped him, since,
transformed him into melancholy lout?

He wanders Elsinore with moans and sighs,
and prattles to himself remarks absurd.
When we meet, he seems not to recognize
his former love, but greets me with rude words.

Can I restore his humor and his sense—
and if they're gone, what is my recompense?

Sonnet Game Triptych: 2. Begging Counsel

Your Honor, like you, I live from the sea—
I trade in precious whale oil and baleen.
Though I know my business, sir, advise me,
how I might find the damndest whale I've seen.

From jaw to tail, this shrewd beast is massive;
its leathery skin, a ghost's unholy white.
Don't that think my life-long search is passive—
I hunt this Moby Dick both day and night.

I've chased this curséd creature each season
that I've sailed on the oceanic tides.
I'm asking, sir, in the blest name of reason:
you must tell me where this Leviathan hides.

My life is incomplete until I catch
this insolent whale, who thinks he is my match.

Sonnet Game Triptych: 3. Mariner's Request

Call me Ishmael, if you please, my lord:
a seaman, employed on a whaling craft.
Last November, I sailed from New Bedford—
I fear my captain, sir, has since gone daft.

The *Pequot* is a tight and tidy ship
with as fine a crew as you ever spied;
to catch right whales, we're skilled and we're equipped—
but Captain Ahab is not satisfied.

We've oil in barrels; every precious prize
rendered from our catch, yet Ahab commands
we find his white whale. Don't he realize
that men grow restive under such demands?

Me and my mates, we know life on the sea.
Have we some recourse, short of mutiny?

Wordsworth Quintet 1: Her Dwelling was Along my Way
("She Dwelt among the Untrodden Ways")

Her dwelling was along my way
  And so I found her there.
Disguised as Poet, not roué,
  Persuaded her to share

Her maidenhood. Half hidden by
  The damp and mossy stones
Skirts hiked, she soon was ridden by
  Me. Then I left, alone.

Immortalized in verse, her fame,
  Though she has ceased to be—
And Lucy wasn't her real name!
  (Indifferent, that, to me.)

Wordsworth Quintet 2: **Strange Flights of Fancy He Describes**

("Strange Fits of Passion Have I Known")

Strange flights of fancy he describes,
as if of consequence.
This silly tale that he confides
makes less than zero sense.

He tells us that he rode to see
his sweetie pie, one June,
concocting a wild fantasy
about a lethal moon.

What can we make of this excess
of morbid self-indulgence?
He manufactures his distress—
which makes me feel repugnance.

I pray he's not as feckless
as he purports to be.
I wish his were words worth respect—
not such frivolity.

Wordsworth Quintet 3: To his French Mistress
("I Travelled among Unknown Men")

I traveled among unknown men
   In lands beyond the sea
And also knew a woman, there,
   In full carnality.

'T'is past, that episode's delight!
   The daughter that she bore
I recognized as mine, alright,
   And yet I quit that shore.

Though in times past, need did I feel
   To send financial help,
But here in England, could conceal
   Connection to that whelp.

I've left behind that dalliance,
   My prospects here are great!
This history adds to my romance:
   "The Deadbeat Laureate."

Wordsworth Quintet 4: For Marge Benjamin

"The world is too much with us," you declare,
reciting verse youthfully memorized
for future consolation, on advice
of some long-ago teacher. She prepared
you for life's losses; knew you'd not be spared
the sad trajectory of later years:
illness, widowhood. Transcending your fears,
declaiming poetry as potent prayer,
you winnow the essentials of your life,
considering if you should leave behind
your belov'd home, where you'd been belov'd wife.
Your interest in material things subsides;
your longing now is simply to arrive
where incorporeal Beauty still abides.

Wordsworth Quintet 5: Westminster Bridge, January 10, 2014

I'm standing in the city's compass rose
upon a bridge that stretches east and west
above the Thames' north-south. Tourists press
cameras in my hands, then pose below
the world's most famous clock. I do not know
what prompts their journeying, to gather here
near London Eye's carnival atmosphere.

The crowds are motivated, I suppose
by images from movies or TV—
by 0-0-7 and by Dr. Who,
rather than half-remembered poetry.
The ships are gone; tall buildings block the view
of all the domes and theaters; still, for me,
the city's mighty heart beats here, anew.

Walt Whitman Discovers the Internet

The italicized language is Whitman's own, from his poem "Passage to India."

Singing these days, *the great achievements of the present*,
Singing the visible and invisible *works of engineers*,
Hardware and software, *our modern wonders*,
Scores of gigabytes, compressed to pocket-size!
The Old World and the New are *spann'd*,
Our *seas inlaid*, still, with *eloquent gentle wires*.
Find their eloquence yet augmented by satellites
        Orbiting in the no-longer-void of space!
Multiplied by satellite dishes fixed on land,
        Receptive faces turned, each to the other!
Substanceless signals, zooming and bouncing
Through the air, to sound *with thee, O soul*!

Passage to India!
Past-laden, the *projectile form* of History
Still keeps on, our present *impell'd by the past*, drives on,
From the *Indus and Ganges* to the IT hub of Bangalore!
Beyond, to China, awash in microchips, producing, consuming!
Beyond, to archipelagoes of distant islands,
Unnumbered as the stars, their names, even if unknown to me,
Undoubtedly catalogued somewhere online!

So, *eclaircise the myths Asiatic, the primitive fables*.
Bhaghavad Gita, online! The entire Mahabharata, online!
Not you alone ye facts of modern science,
But myths and fables of old, Asia's, Africa's fables!

The deep diving bibles and legends,
The daring plots of poets, the elder religions,
I read them all here! I wander, unencumbered,
In this bright marketplace of faces, thoughts, and goods,
Sacred and profane, crossing borders without passport,
Where the Poetry Foundation democratizes the
Utterances of innumerable souls, living and immortal!
To a region where Rumi himself has a Facebook page
- no more daring poetic plot imaginable!

O you fables spurning the known, eluding the hold
      Of the known, mounting to heaven!
You lofty and dazzling towers, pinnacled,
      Red as roses, burnish'd with gold!
Construct of Ideas unimaginable, spoken in various tongues,
To build again one Tower, with one tongue,
Babel renewed, not to be again unraveled!

Passage to India!
Lo, soul, seest thou not God's purpose from the first?
The earth to be spann'd, connected by network,
Fiber optic, wireless, SANs and PANs and LANs,
Data humming endlessly across time zones,
Ungoverned and ungovernable, information set free!
The races, neighbors, to marry and be given in marriage,
Importuning would-be brides, from Russia and Ukraine!
Handsome people of every sex, wishing to become Skype contacts!

Passage to India!
The oceans to be cross'd, the distant brought near,
Nigerian millionaires with cash-flow problems, seeking help!
Attractive new persons, drawn to me, eagerly sending
Friend requests, translation possible at the click of a mouse!
All affection shall be fully responded to, the secret shall be told,
All these separations shall be taken up and hook'd and link'd together.
United, in ecstasy, myself, all races, our neighbors, all history,
Joined together, now grown incandescent,
Our past and present, vibrating to the frequency of thee, o soul!

(Sic) Transit (Gloria Mundi)
This one can pretty much be sung to the tune of "The Streets of Laredo."

At the Duty-Free shop inside Dublin Airport,
middle aged women are employed to pour
samples of liquors in small plastic vessels
offered to travelers urged to buy more.

One little stand I saw caught my attention—
it advertised a drink which was called "Coole Swan."
May the public visit there? I asked the lady.
Visit where? she asked me; I answered, *Coole Park.*

Well, I wouldn't know, dear, she bluntly admitted.
It's something to do with a poet, who's dead—
a famous one, though - Mr. Yeats, his name is.
I nodded. *I think I've heard of him,* I said.

Oh Poet! Oh Senator! Nobel Laureate!
You shaped your nation's life, when it was new;
determined its cultural future would be great—
rest easy! Know that Ireland remembers you.

Easter 1916, Reimagined for Maud

My dear Willie,
No I don't like your poem, it isn't worthy of you & above all it isn't worthy of
the subject - ....it isn't quite sincere enough for you who have studied philosophy
and know something of history know quite well that sacrifice never yet turned a
heart to stone though it has immortalised many & through it alone can
mankind rise to God- ....There are beautiful lines in your poem, as there are
in all you write but it is not a great WHOLE, a living thing which our race
would treasure & repeat, such as a poet like you might have given to your
nation....
From a letter written by Maud Gonne to William Butler Yeats,
November 8, 1916

I think the common condition of our life is hatred – I know this is so with me
– irritation with public or private events or persons.
William Butler Yeats

I would see them at close of day,
With stiff or angry faces,
Self-proclaimed leaders of our grey
City's unhappy masses.
Perhaps a curt nod of the head
towards men who aimed spiteful words
At *me* – for, with all they had said
What choice but fight with words?
With a thought to hold my own
Or, better, to press forth my side
In this unmannerly town,
Certain it was worthwhile to fight
Against detractors of my work
Back when motley was still worn:
But all changed suddenly—
My discourse must rise beyond scorn.

That woman was reprieved
And so needs little praise;
The "Countess Markievicz,"
Sligo's pride, in her day.
Lovely as a gazelle

Destined to be a prize—
But wed a feckless Pole.
One tried to ostracize
Me, who lacked Irish tongue;
Another, a devoted Gael,
Of all this lot was the one
I liked best. At Saint Enda's school
He taught, and wrote poetry well,
Showing both feeling and skill.
Of the last, there's much to tell
Yet I hesitate to speak ill
Of him, whose prominent part
Was poking his foxy face
Near to those dearest to my heart.
Therefore must I in good grace
Pay him due credit in my song,
In the part for which I'd been spurned:
Hero, certainly,
Demi-god in green uniform.

What, then, is a heart's purpose?
Who can entirely know
Where motive finds focus?
Few possess gifts like my own
To paint a landscape in flux
In contrast with fixéd stone.
Had that stone been heart, once,
Before breaking a stream's flow,
What alteration transformed it?
Of all the systems I know
My faith is in enchantment.
Willful souls can transform life's flow—
Halt clouds; change course of stream
Conjure a moor-hen's call,
Create the world that they dream—
Mages, in the midst of it all.

Misguided zealotry
Can turn tender hearts against
Custom's ceremonies;

Breed minds quick to take offense
At wise liberality.
History may not condemn
Their dreams or stridency
For by their death these men
Achieved by alchemy
Their Philosopher's Stone:
Even most base, changed utterly.
Challenged is England's throne
Unsettled its long scepter;
Its rule not yet undone,
But altered by these specters,
Who waged a battle half won.
For McDonough and MacBride
As with Connolly and Pearse,
Transfigured as they died
Into heroes of verse;
In memory of men,
Wherever green is worn,
Sacrifice told again
In terrible beauty, reborn.

Ballade, for the Duke of Orleans

Charles, Duke of Orleans, wrote poetry before and during his 24 years of captivity in England, after being taken prisoner at the Battle of Agincourt. Released by the English in 1440, he became a great patron of the arts, once setting a competition – known as the "concours de Blois" – in which he asked poets of his day to compose *ballades* with the first line, "Je meurs de soif auprès de la fontaine" – "I die of thirst next to the fountain." Manuscripts survive of *ballades* composed with this first line by Villon, Montbeton, Robertet, Bertault de Villesbresme, Gilles des Ourmes, and Jehan and Simonnet Caillau.

I die of thirst, here, by the fountain's pour
of refreshment, and will not lift my head
to drink salvation. As I've done before,
I turn away and close my lips instead.
Defying my survival's deep instinct,
I find a satisfaction that's perverse—
long a hunger artist, who would yet drink,
now I'm perfecting the rare art of thirst.

I will not quaff the love from lovers' eyes
just as I would no sweet embrace consume.
Such self-denial kindles your surprise—
would I then go, uncherished, to the tomb?
Although concupiscence exerts its pull,
I say again, as I have from the first:
completely empty far surpasses full,
and I'm perfecting the rare art of thirst.

Some hasten to me with a silver cup
or offer me a great goblet of gold,
as if metallic shine might bid me sup;
somehow entice the yielding I withhold.
What do I care for this poor worldly dross?
Just minerals – none are better or worse.
Please understand that I will feel no loss,
for I'm perfecting the rare art of thirst.

The fountain's music is my sustenance,
its random plashings suffice to revive
my ebbing self. See how the waters dance,
emprismed and begilded! I survive

to see its transient splendor on display;
to watch, undrinking, a blessing - not curse,
as I progress along the lofty way
to perfecting that rarest art of thirst.

Please do not think that I merit your praise,
nor judge renunciation's worth accrued.
This discipline is naught you can appraise,
and your miscalculation if you do.
My life's work has become a hollow thing;
a vessel, with no content to disperse -
but strike its edge, and you will make it ring -
clear note of my ultimate art of thirst.

Envoi
There is no more to say; I've made my case.
Don't be repulsed, neither imitate me;
my spirit rises as flesh is effaced,
traded in hope of song's eternity.

Shall I Marry Poetry?

Should I speak the vows?
Can I honor, and remain irreverent?
Do I have it in me to obey?

Is love as satisfying over the breakfast
table as it was in the back of
my old car? As oddly durable?

Shall I take the risk of devotion?
Or better to carry on in the familiar
way, to say I'm working late

when instead, I'm out with you,
a little giddy from red wine,
flirting madly over long-stemmed glasses?

Will I love you as much over coffee cups?
Will you still have as much to say to me?

ABOUT THE AUTHOR

Denise Provost served for many years in local government and for almost fifteen years in the Massachusetts House of Representatives. She has published in such journals as *Ibbetson Street, Muddy River Poetry Review, qarrtsiluni, Quadrille, Poetry Porch's Sonnet Scroll, Sanctuary, Light Quarterly*, and in numerous Bagel Bard anthologies. She received the New England Poetry Club's Samuel Washington Allen Award in 2021, and the Best Love Sonnet Award from the Maria C. Faust Sonnet Competition in 2012. Her chapbook *Curious Peach* was published by *Ibbetson Street Press* in 2019.

CPSIA information can be obtained
at www.ICGtesting.com
Printed in the USA
BVHW032358070122
625759BV00001B/55